ALL ABOUT HORSES

BIG IDEAS: HIGH BEGINNER

DOROTHY ZEMACH

WAYZGOOSE PRESS

ISBN: 978-1-961953-27-7

CONTENTS

INTRODUCTION

This book is divided into sections. You can read the sections in any order, and you don't have to read all of them.

A note about vocabulary

There is a lot of new vocabulary to learn to talk about horses! This is true in any language. Even native speakers of a language have to learn specialized vocabulary for specific subjects—like horses. I decided not to put a long list of every horse word here because I don't think that's a useful or efficient way to learn vocabulary. Instead, some new words are presented in different sections, especially in the first section, **Meet the Horse**. At the end of the first two chapters, *General Information* and *Riding a Horse*, there is a short vocabulary review section.

When a new word is introduced, it's presented in ***bold italics***. That means it's a useful or important word, and I recommend learning it. You will probably also see other words that you don't know—you can check a dictionary if you want, but you do not need to pay special attention to those words. In addition, the important new words you have to learn are often repeated again and again throughout the book. This makes them easier to remember.

Some learners like to write new words in a notebook, or keep them in a list on their phones. Others make flashcards, which you can do on paper or with online programs like Quizlet. Or—just keep reading books about horses! That is how I learned horse vocabulary when I was a child. I have put some recommendations for famous children's horse stories in this book that you could read in English.

I hope you enjoy learning more about horses!

Dorothy Zemach

PART 1

MEET THE HORSE

If you like horses, you probably already know a lot about them. But maybe you don't know much horse vocabulary in English. And horses need a lot of vocabulary! We use special words to talk about what horses look like, how they act, what they wear, where they live, and what people do with them. This section will teach you a lot of special vocabulary for talking about horses. But don't worry--you don't have to learn it all at one time. You can check this section again whenever you need to.

1 GENERAL INFORMATION

A horse is *mammal*—the same type of animal as a dog, a cat, and a human. They have warm blood, they are covered with hair (called a *coat*), and they give live birth (that means, they don't lay eggs).

But a horse is more than just a mammal.

A horse is a *herd* animal: that means that, in the wild, it lives in a group (called a herd). If you drive by a field of horses, you will probably see them standing together. In addition, a horse herd has one leader and several followers. The leader is a *stallion* (a male horse), and the followers are mostly *mares* (female horses) and *colts* (young male horses) and *fillies* (young female horses). When the colts grow up, some of them leave the herd and become leaders of their own herds.

In the wild, horses eat grass and small plants. They also eat fruits and berries, if they can find them. Walking around and eating grass is called *grazing*. To get enough food, wild horses graze more than 15 hours a day! In the winter, when it is harder to find grass, horses will eat other parts of plants, including leaves and the bark of trees. When people keep horses, they feed their horses hay and grains inside the *barn*, and let them graze on fresh grass outside. Some people give their horses treats such as apples, pears, or carrots. However, you shouldn't give horses sugar (even though they like it). It's not good for their teeth or their general health. Horses need plenty of fresh water, and they also need salt. Wild horses find salt outdoors on rocks and plants. Sometimes they travel a long way to find salt! People who keep horses in barns give them pieces of salt to lick, called salt blocks.

Horses are active during the day and sleep at night. You might see wild horses sleeping on their feet instead of lying down. This keeps them safe from *predators*—other animals that might try to eat them, like a wolf or a cougar. But horses can sleep lying down, and they often do this in barns.

Horses have very good eyesight and hearing. They can only breathe through their nose, and not also through their mouth (like humans can). They have a good sense of smell. Horses are intelligent, and they can be trained to do many things. They can recognize different people, and will remember if that person was kind to them or not.

People began *domesticating* horses about 6000 years ago. That sounds like a long time ago, but the dog was domesticated about 14,000 years ago! Even the cat was domesticated before the horse, about 8,500 years ago. Horses have been used for work, like plowing fields for farmers or pulling wagons, to carry soldiers in battle, and for transportation. And, of course, people ride horses for pleasure. In sports, horses are used for polo and *equestrian* sports such as jumping and racing. Horses are even used to help people feel better, such as sick children or people who feel nervous or sad. These horses are called therapy horses.

A horse can live for 30 or more years if it has good food, enough water, a safe place to sleep, and healthcare. In the wild, horses live around 15-20 years. It's harder for wild horses to find enough food, and when they get older, they might be attacked by predators.

Vocabulary

Do you remember what these words mean? Can you recognize them when you are reading? Can you use them in an original sentence? If you need more practice, read this section again or check a dictionary.

- stallion
- mare
- colt
- filly
- herd
- barn
- graze
- predator
- domesticate
- equestrian

Parts of a horse

As you can see, there are special names for different parts of a horse. Unless you own a horse and need to take care of it in English, you don't need to know most of these words —but you might be interested! However, you should know *mane*, *tail*, *withers*, and *hoof*. Can you find those in the picture?

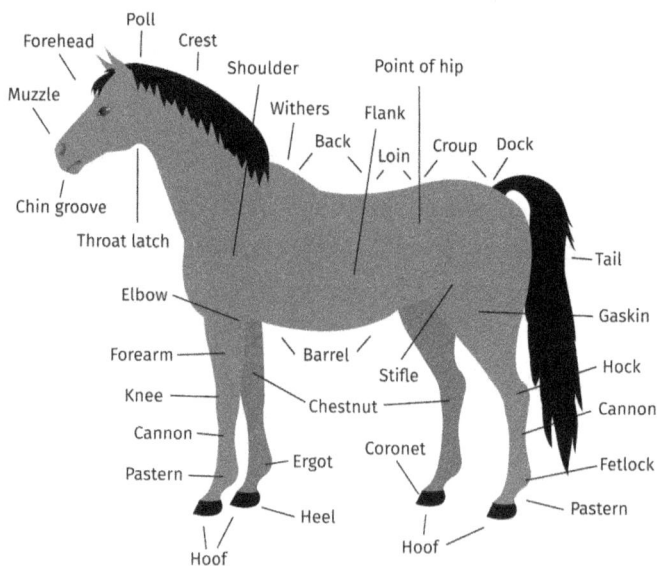

2 RIDING A HORSE

Equestrian activities and sports are very popular. People enjoy riding horses. When a horse is about 3-4 years old, it can learn to wear a saddle and bridle, and then to carry a person on its back. Both the horse and the rider need a lot of practice, though!

Equipment for riding a horse is called *tack*, and it is kept in a *tack room*. The most important pieces of tack are the *saddle*, the *bridle*, and the *halter*. There are many different kinds of saddles and bridles. What kind you choose depends on the horse and on what kind of riding you want to do.

A typical saddle has a *girth*—a long strap that goes around the horse's stomach—and *stirrups* of metal or leather for the rider to put their feet in. Before you put a saddle on a horse's pack, put down a *saddle pad* or *saddle blanket*, so the horse feels more comfortable.

The bridle goes on the horse's head. A metal *bit* goes inside its mouth, and the rider holds the *reins* in their hands. The rider uses the reins to tell the horse when to turn, stop, and go backwards, but a good rider gives the horse many different kinds of signals from their legs, their body position, and even their voice.

A horse wearing some tack: a saddle pad, a saddle, and a bridle

A halter looks a little like a bridle, but it doesn't have a bit, and it doesn't have reins. Instead, you can attach a piece of rope to it and lead the horse where you want it to go.

Riders also need some special equipment. You need strong shoes or boots, long pants, and a helmet. Even very good riders sometimes fall off when their horses get scared. Horses can trip and fall. It's good to be prepared so that you are protected if you or your horse fall.

Most riders take riding lessons, and advanced riders

might work with a special trainer who can help them become better partners with their horse.

A horse has different *gaits*, or ways of moving. When a horse walks, it moves each foot separately. When it *trots*, it moves two legs at the same time. When it *canters*, it moves its back legs together and its front legs separately. When it *gallops*, it moves each foot separately—but a gallop is a lot faster than a walk! The easiest way to understand these gaits is to check videos on YouTube. There are many, many videos like this. At the time this book was published, this link showed very nice examples of both Western and English style riding of the walk, trot, canter: https://www.youtube.com/watch?v=G80Tn-Hy2tE

There are other gaits, but the walk, trot, canter, and gallop are the most common.

There are also many styles of riding! The main styles are English and Western. English and Western styles use different saddles and different bridles, and they also feel different for the rider (and the horse!).

Here are some main differences:

- **Saddle**: The English saddle is smaller and lighter. You will see English saddles on horses that jump in horse shows. The Western saddle was designed for workers in the American West to sit in all day, so it is heavier and more comfortable to ride in for a long time. The Western saddle also has a pommel, which can be used to tie a rope to, or for the rider to hold onto.

- **Reins**: The Western reins are held in one hand, and English reins in both hands. To ask a horse to turn right, with Western reins, you pull them against the left side of the horse's neck. With English reins, you can pull gently on the right rein, although it's better to use your legs and body weight to tell the horse what you want.
- **Riders' clothes**: Although both English and Western riders usually wear boots or strong shoes, long pants, and a helmet, the styles can look very different. Sometimes Western riders wear a cowboy hat. If you have watched any equestrian events in the Olympics, you saw English-style tack and riders.

Vocabulary

Do you remember the meaning of these words?

- bit
- bridle
- canter
- gait
- gallop
- halter
- reins
- saddle
- stirrup
- tack
- trot

3 HORSE COLORS

Horses are different shades of black, brown, and white. However, these colors have special names! Some are used only for horses, and some are used for other animals too. There are also special words for the markings some horses have on their coats. Some colors can be found in many different horse *breeds* (types of animals), and some breeds have only a few colors.

There are many different horse colors, but here are some of the most common:

- **Black:** Some breeds of horses are almost never black, and other breeds are often black (like the Friesian horse on the cover of this book). Two of the most famous children's books about horses were about black horses: *Black Beauty* and *The Black Stallion.*
- **Chestnut:** A chestnut horse is brown, with a mane and tail that are the same color or lighter.

A chestnut horse's coat can be light brown, red, or a medium brown.

- **Bay:** A bay horse is also brown, but darker than a chestnut horse, and it has a black mane, tail, and feet. Bay is the most common horse color.
- **Palomino:** This horse is golden in color, with a white mane and tail. Many people think palominos are very beautiful, so they are popular show animals. A golden-colored horse with a black mane, tail, and feet is called a **buckskin**.
- **Gray:** Very few horses are really completely **white**; instead they are called **gray**, because they have dark skin under their coats. But they still look white, and people still use that word for them.
- **Roan:** A **roan** horse is covered with many spots. Roan horses can be different colors, such as brown or gray, but they all have some white hairs mixed in, that give them their spotted look.
- **Pinto:** A **pinto** horse is white with large black or brown spots—in fact, the word *pinto* comes from the Spanish word for "spotted." Pintos are popular in the United States and Canada. In British English, sometimes a pinto horse is called a "colored" horse.

Are you interested in other horse colors? Here are some to research online. Make sure you look for photos as well as descriptions:

- Appaloosa (this is also a horse breed)
- Dun
- Piebald
- Skewbald

Some people think that the color of a horse affects its personality. Some people believe that black horses are strong, white horses are gentle, and chestnut horses are lively or have a hot temper. Other people don't believe that at all. In fact, no scientific study has shown that the color of a horse's coat affects its personality. However, the way people behave around horses can influence them. So if you think a horse is gentle, you might behave gently with that horse—and then it becomes gentle. If you know people who own horses, ask them what they think. They will probably have a lot of stories!

Two pinto horses playing in the snow

PART 2
HORSE BLOODS

Horses are divided into three main categories: Hot bloods, warm bloods, and cold bloods.

Of course, the actual temperature of horses' blood is the same. Horses are mammals, and they are all warm-blooded animals. A hot blood does not have blood that is hotter than the blood of a cold blood! So do not take these words too literally. These terms really divide horses by size and personality.

Here is some useful vocabulary for talking about horse breeds:

- *Sire*: Like a "father," the sire is a male parent horse. This can also be used as a verb: *My horse sired a beautiful black colt.*
- *Dam*: Like a "mother," this dam is the female

parent horse. However, dam is not used as a verb.

- *Foal*: a young horse. A foal can be either a colt or a filly. This can also be a verb, meaning "to give birth to": *That mare foaled a filly in the spring.*

Imagine that the foal Star Bright has a sire named Silver Moon and a dam named Golden Sun. We say that Star Bright is **out of** Golden Sun **by** Silver Moon. That is, a colt or filly is *out of* the dam *by* the sire. When you read information about famous racehorses, the horse's parents are often mentioned like this. *The famous Australian racehorse Phar Lap, by Night Raid out of Entreaty, died suddenly in California for unknown reasons.*

4 HOT BLOODS

Hot-blooded horses like this Arabian make good race horses.

Hot-blooded horses sensitive and intelligent, and they are very energetic and active. They mostly developed in the Middle East, and were traditionally used for war, travel, and companionship. Today they are often used for horse racing and pleasure riding.

Arabian

Arabian horses are one of the oldest breeds. Many people think they are one of the most beautiful breeds. They have small heads but large eyes, and they have smaller bodies than some other horse breeds, between 145 and 155 cm high. They have short, straight backs and strong bones, and they hold their tails high. They learn quickly and are loyal to their riders if they are well cared for. They are especially famous for their *endurance*—this means that they can walk and run long distances for a long time.

Thoroughbred

Thoroughbred horses were bred for racing. In fact, every thoroughbred horse descended from one of three famous Arabian stallions:

- The **Byerley Turk** (about 1680 –1703). Probably born in Turkey (nobody really knows for sure), he was used as a war horse in Europe and Ireland. Later his owner, Captain Robert Byerley, brought him to England.
- The **Darley Arabian** (about 1700 – 1730). He was bought in Syria and brought to England by Thomas Darley as a gift for his brother. He sired

many famous racehorses. Most thoroughbreds are related to the Darley Arabian.

- The **Godolphin Barb** (about 1724 – 1753). He was born in Yemen or Morocco and then was probably moved to Syria. From there he was given as a gift to the king of France, who did not think he was very special and used him only for work. He was then bought by someone in England, and changed owners a few times before he was bought by the Earl of Godolphin. There is a good children's book about the Godolphin Barb called *King of the Wind*, by Marguerite Henry, which mixes fiction with facts. Some of his famous descendants include the racehorses Man O'War and Seabiscuit.

5 WARM BLOODS

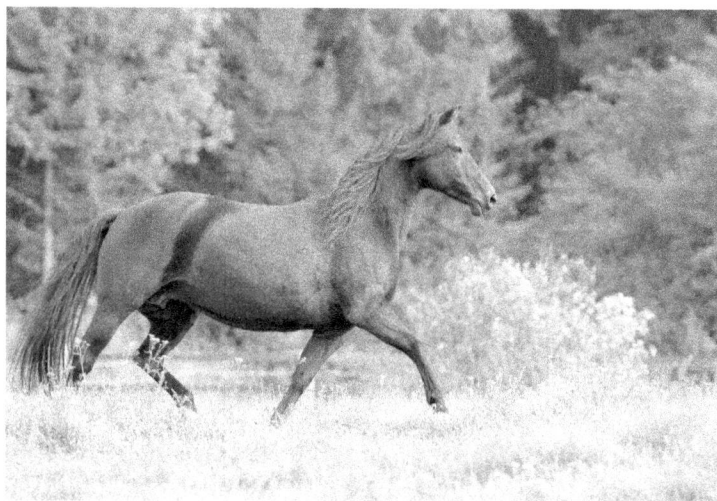

Warmbloods like this Morgan are popular horses for riding.

Warmblood horses are medium-sized horses that are often used for sport, such as polo, jumping, and dressage (a type of competition where riders show how highly trained their horses are).

Hanoverian

Hanoverians are known for being gentle and easy to train, and they are popular with people learning to ride. They look elegant, but they are also very strong. For these reasons, they make excellent show horses for jumping and dressage. Many of the horses you see jumping in the Olympic games are Hanoverians. This horse is one of the oldest types of warmblood horses and came from Germany. The breed became established in the mid-1800s.

Hanoverians are also good at the sport of *eventing*. This sport combines three different types of competition: dressage, jumping, and cross-country (you can read more about these competitions later in this book). Eventing competitions can last for one, two, or even three days. During the cross-country race, horses jump over fences and small rivers, but instead of in a closed show ring, like for show jumping, they run across open land.

Morgan

Morgan horses were developed in the United States. The first Morgan horse, named Figure, was born in in the state of Massachusetts. Nobody is 100% sure who his sire and dam were! Most people believe that he had blood from the Byerly Turk line and the Godolphin Arabian line (see the section on Arab horses, in hot bloods), and the American Quarter Horse Association is mostly sure that his sire was the English thoroughbred True Briton. Other historians believe his sire was a thoroughbred named

Beautiful Bay. So his complete history will always be a mystery.

Justin Morgan was a singing teacher and music composer who lived in the state of Vermont. He was also very interested in breeding horses. In 1792, Morgan traveled to Massachusetts to collect some money he was owed. Instead of money, he agreed to take two horses—including a 3-year-old bay colt. That was Figure.

Figure was medium-sized but very strong and fast. He also had a very calm and pleasant personality. He became famous for his speed and strength, competing against larger horses and winning. He became known as "Justin Morgan's horse," and that is why today his descendants are known as Morgan horses.

Morgan offering Figure for breeding: people would pay him to have Figure be the sire of new foals. People found that Figure's colts and fillies looked like him, were strong like him, and had has personality. Morgan horses were used for racing and pulling carriages, and they are still very popular horses for riding.

6 COLD BLOODS

Shire horses were often used for farm work.

Cold-blooded horses are typically large and gentle. They are often used for work such as farming or pulling carriages. Cold blooded horses came from colder, northern countries.

They are known for their strength and their calm person-
alities.

Shire

The shire is one of the largest and tallest horses in the
world! It is a type of *draft* horse – a horse that is used for
work such as pulling carts or wagons or even canal boats or
farm work. These days, more farmers use tractors and
other machines that horses to plow their fields, but draft
horses are still popular because of their looks.

In fact, since the 1920s, the appearance of the Shire has
changed. People bred them with Clydesdales, another
breed of draft horse, so that their feathers became lighter
and softer over time.

Feathers? On a horse? Yes! Look at the feet of the shire
horse at the beginning of this section. Do you see the long
hairs just above the hooves? Those are called *feathers*, and
we say that draft horses have *feathering*. Shire horse
feathers used to be thick and rough, but today they are
light and silky.

Shire horses have wide, short backs and strong shoulders. They are calm and patient, and they don't get scared
easily. It is possible to ride a Shire horse, but it's more
common for them to be used for work (such as pulling
carriages for tourists to ride in) or for shows and competitions.

Friesian

Look at the cover of this book again. That beautiful black horse is a Friesian. The name comes from the place the breed comes from: Friesland, in the Netherlands. It is thought that people were riding Friesian horses there as early as the 4th century! Friesian horses were used for both work and riding. Medieval knights rode Friesians, who were strong enough to carry a soldier wearing armor.

Today Friesian horses are popular because of their elegant looks. They have large eyes, small ears, strong bodies, long manes and tails, and lovely feathering at their feet. They have **high action** – that means they pick their feet up high when they walk, trot, or canter. They are friendly and intelligent, and they make good riding horses. They are also a popular choice for dressage competitions.

All Friesians are black. To be registered as an official Friesian horse, it cannot have any white marks except a small white star on the forehead.

PART 3

EQUESTRIAN SPORTS AND COMPETITIONS

Many people love sports, and people who love horses often love doing sports with horses! There are many different types of sports that you can do with a horse, and this book is not long enough to describe them all. At the end of the chapter, I will mention some other sports for you to look up on your own. For example, can you guess what **horse vaulting** is?

7 HORSE RACES

Horse racing is sometimes called "the sport of kings."

Horse racing is a very old sport. Many ancient civilizations such as those in Egypt, Arabia, Babylon, Greece, and Rome raced horses.

The simplest type of horse race is around a *race track*. The track is usually shaped like an oval. All horses start at the same time, and the horse that gets to the end of the track first wins. Of course, a horse closest to the inside of the track has less distance to run than the horses that are further away. So when the race begins, often the horses' riders—called *jockeys*—try to move their horses to the inside.

Of course, there are many different types of horse racing, including:

- **flat racing**, where horses run from start to finish over flat ground
- **jump racing**, where horses both run and jump over different obstacles, (often called *jumps*) such as fences, gates, bushes, or small ponds. A jump race is often called a steeplechase in the UK.
- **harness racing**, where horses pull their riders in a small cart
- **endurance racing**, where horses race for a long distance and a long time, over open countryside with many obstacles
- and many more!

In addition, in each of those categories there are many variations. A flat race can be short or long. The racetrack can be straight or an oval, and made of grass, dirt, or even synthetic materials. Flat races are the most popular worldwide.

In jump racing, horses are judged both on how fast they race and on whether they can jump over the obstacle. If their feet touch part of the jump or if they knock the jump over, they lose points. You can see some good examples of jump racing in the Summer Olympics. This is one of the few sports where men and women compete together. You can easily find videos of past competitions online. Watch a few and see if you can tell which horses are going to do the best. Everyone hopes that the horse will not *refuse* (stop in front of a jump or run around it)! This sport is often called *show jumping*.

Often at horse races, people can *bet* on the winner. That is, they pay some money and guess if the horse they choose will win, or come in first, second, or third. If they guess right, they will win more money. If they guess wrong, then they lose the. money that they bet. Betting on horse races involves a lot of money. For example, in the state of Kentucky in the US, betting on horse races gives jobs to about 24,000 people! It earns about $1.9 billion a year, and $115 million in taxes. Kentucky is home to the Kentucky Derby, one of the most famous flat races.

One interesting system in horse races is **handicapping**. Before the race, judges decide which horses they think are the strongest and fastest, and then they make those horses carry extra weight, called a *handicap*. They even figure out the weight of the *jockey* (rider). The handicap system is supposed to make the race more fair by making it more difficult for the best horses. Do you think that is more fair, or less fair? Not all people agree! It does make the race more even, so it is harder to guess who will win. And that means more money will be won—and lost—at betting.

8 HORSE SHOWS

Show jumping is a popular type of competition

This is a big category! There are many kinds of horse shows. You have already read a bit about show jumping, and this is one of the most common types of events at a horse show. But many other competitions happen at a horse show too.

Beginning and advanced riders can compete against each other to show their riding skills. Beginners are usually asked to walk, trot, and canter, to show that they can control their horse well.

In North America, competitions for horses who use a Western saddle are common. Often these events feature some aspect of farm or ranch work. For example, a calf (baby cow) or other farm animal is put into the arena, and the horse and rider must work together to chase the animal, catch it, and then tie it (of course, only the rider is tying!). The event is timed, and the rider who can catch and tie the animal the fastest is the winner. Sometimes horses and riders work in teams.

Calf roping

There are also barrel races, where horses race around

many barrels. Again, they are timed, and the fastest horse wins. There are competitions called pulls, where horses compete to pull something very heavy, such as a tree log. The horse who can pull the heaviest item wins.

There are even games at some horse shows! In the UK (and in fact, in just about every English-speaking country outside of the United States), horse shows called gymkhanas feature races, jumping, and games. There are many kinds of games, such as racing around poles, carrying an egg in a spoon (without dropping it!), and picking up flags from a barrel. The games are for fun, of course, but they also test the rider's skill. Search for videos of "gymkhana games" online to see some fun competitions!

As beginners, people compete for ribbons or cups. At top levels, people can also win money.

Other Horse Sports

Horses are part of other sports, too. There's **polo**, where teams of people on horseback try to hit a ball through the other team's goal. There is also **horseball**, which is a more recent sport that is kind of like basketball on horseback. If you are very adventurous, perhaps you would like to try **buzkashi**, which is played in Afghanistan and other Central Asian countries, where teams try to put a a dead goat or calf in a goal.

Horses also compete in Western shows called **rodeos**, and they're a popular animal in the **circus**. If you're interested in gymnastics and acrobatics, you will like **horse**

vaulting, a way of doing gymnastics on top of a horse— while it is moving!

A young performer horse vaulting

9 DRESSAGE

A horse and rider in a dressage competition

Dressage is a special kind of horse competition. The word "dressage" comes from French, and means "training." It is a competition to see how skillfully a rider can ask the horse to do some difficult things.

If you are sitting in the audience, it can be very hard to see how the dressage rider sends signals to the horse. Usually, they are using their leg muscles and their weight to let the horse know what to do. Some of the actions that dressage horses do are almost like horse gymnastics. Dressage is an Olympic sport, so you can watch videos of former competitions. See if you can figure out how the rider is communicating to their horse!

Dressage has been practiced as a sport and an art since at least the mid-1500s. A good dressage rider also trains their horse, so they work with the same horse for many years.

Some of the most famous dressage horses are the Lipizzaner horses of Europe. They developed in the Italian city of Lipica (which is spelled Lipizza in Italian), and were bred and trained in different European countries including Slovenia and Austria. Lipizzaner horses are strong and powerful, and they live a long time. Almost all of them are gray. They were descended from the Godolphin Barb (see the section on hot-blooded horses) and other Arabian horses. Today, every Lipizzaner horse is descended from one of eight original Lipizzaner horses.

Today, the most famous Lipizzaner horses are found at the Spanish Riding School in Vienna, Austria. If you visit, you may be able to watch a free practice session!

There have been many books and movies about these special horses, including the children's book *White Stallion of Lipizza*, by Marguerite Henry, the mystery/adventure story *Airs Above the Ground*, by Marguerite Henry, and the Disney movie *Miracle of the White Stallions*, about a plot during World War II to steal the horses, and how they were rescued.

One of the famous Lipizzaner stallions from the Spanish Riding School

PART 4

HORSE STORIES

People who love horses love reading about special horses. Some of them really lived, and some of them are fictional, living only in books. In this section, you'll learn about some famous horses from history, and then I'll tell you about some famous horse stories (some fictional, some not) that you can find and read on your own.

10 FAMOUS REAL HORSES

Here are some horses that really lived.

Man O' War

Man O' War is one of the most famous racehorses of all time. He has been called the "best racehorse of the 20th century" by several sports magazines and newspapers.

Man O' War was an American Thoroughbred who was born in 1917, out of Mahubah by Fair Play. Both his sire and his dam were either racehorses themselves or parents who were. Man O' War was a large, powerful chestnut horse with a white star and a stripe on his head. His original owner, August Belmont, sold Man O' War because he couldn't easily work with racehorses during World War I (1914-1918). A man named Samuel Riddle, a businessman and racehorse owner, bought the colt for $5000.

Man O' War was a difficult horse at first. He was wild

and strong, and often threw his exercise riders. His trainer, Louis Feustal, used to work with August Belmont, and when Belmont stopped keeping racehorses, he first raced horses by himself and then went to work for Samuel Riddle. Feustal worked hard to get Man O' War calm and steady enough for jockeys to ride him safely. Man O' War's *groom* (the person who cleans a horse's barn, feeds him, and takes care of him) became the horse's friend. He fed him oranges as a special treat, and Man O' War learned to carry his hat!

Man O' War started racing as a two-year old, and he easily won his first race. And his second race. In fact, Man O' War won every race in his life except one, and his jockey believed that a major reason for his one loss was a mistake. The man who started the race was waiting for all the horses to be ready. But Man O' War was turning around when the starter began the race, and so Man O' War started just a little behind. He came in second, just behind a hors named Upset. Was that the only reason he lost? We will never know, of course, but Man O' War continued to win many famous and difficult races, and he beat Upset four more times.

Clever Hans

How smart is a horse? Can a horse think? Can a horse do math? Many people thought that Clever Hans could!

Hans was the name of a horse in Germany who belonged to Wilhelm van Osten, a math teacher who also trained horses. Van Osten said that he had taught Hans to add, subtract, multiply, and divide—and also to tell time as well as read, spell, and understand German.

To show how Hans could add, for example, van Osten would ask a question (in German) such as "What is six plus four?" Then Hans would tap his hoof ten times, to show that the answer was ten. Sometimes van Osten would show Hans the question or problem written down, in German, for Hans to read and answer in the same way.

The German Board of Education decided to investigate Clever Hans and van Osten. They tried several experiments to see if Hans could really think, including having someone else (not van Osten) ask the questions. They found that if van Osten or another person asked a question, and knew the answer, and Clever Hans could see the person asking the question, Clever Hans got the right answer 89% of the time. That's a B+ for the horse!

However... if the questioner did not know the answer to the question, or if Clever Hans could not see the questioner, then Clever Hans was right only 6% of the time.

Clever Hans was not doing math—or telling time or reading or spelling. He was closely watching the person asking the question. The questioner changed his body language just at the point of the correct answer. Imagine Clever Hans counting to ten, while the questioner watches. He taps his hoof. One, two, three, four, five, six, seven, eight, nine... and here the questioner holds his breath, or perhaps raises his shoulders a little, or perhaps his expression changes. THAT is what Clever Hans was reacting to.

As long as the questioner knew the answer, Hans could work out what that was 89% of the time.

So even though Clever Hans could not read or do math, he was indeed very clever!

Trigger

Trigger (1965, one of the most famous horses in television and movies, was a beautiful palomino horse who belonged to American singer and actor Roy Rogers. At first his owners said his sire was a thoroughbred and his dam an unregistered horse but of palomino coloring. Later, some researchers claimed that Trigger's sire was a palomino Morgan horse or possibly a Thoroughbred/Morgan cross.

Rogers acted in almost 90 movies, usually as a cowboy, and had his own TV show called The Roy Rogers Show, which included his wife, Dale Evans, Trigger, and his dog, Bullet. In fact, you can find many full-length episodes of this show on YouTube: just search for "Roy Rogers Show." They are in black and white, and have many scenes of Western riding. If the actors speak too fast for you at first, turn on the captions and read at the same time. They also use some old-fashioned slang. But even if the grammar is sometimes complex, the story lines are pretty simple and easy to understand. It's a nice look at the western United States in the 1950s. History and horses! Each episode ends with Roy and Dale singing their most famous song, "Happy Trails" as they ride away on their horses.

Trigger (was not originally named "Trigger." That's okay

—Roy Rogers (1911-1998) was not originally named "Roy Rogers"! Rogers was born Leonard Franklin Slye, but changed his name to something easier to remember when he started acting. First he was called Dick Weston, but soon changed to Roy Rogers, which he kept all his life. Trigger was named Golden Cloud. When Rogers met him, he had already acted in one movie, *The Adventures of Robin Hood*. Rogers used Trigger for many of his movies, and loved him so much that he bought him from the movie studio.

Rogers, however, acted in so many movies and made so many public appearances that it was too much work for just one horse. Trigger was actually three main horses, and sometimes some stunt doubles (just as human actors sometimes get stunt doubles to do very dangerous scenes). The other horses were called Trigger for the public. In private, the two used the most were named Little Trigger and Trigger Jr. Little Trigger was a lighter color than Golden Cloud, and he had four white feet (called **stockings**) instead of one, like Golden Cloud—but almost everyone believed that there was only one horse playing Trigger. Little Trigger was the smartest of the Trigger horses, and he learned over 150 tricks, including knocking on doors, untying ropes, and walking on just his two hind legs. Trigger (well, Little Trigger) had such good manners that Rogers could take him into hotels and even hospitals, where Rogers and Trigger would meet with sick children to cheer them up.

Trigger (well, the Triggers) made 82 movies and 100 TV episodes, and Trigger is still called "the smartest horse in the movies." He even had his own comic book series, called *Roy Rogers' Trigger*!

If you check online for some old Roy Rogers movies or episodes from his TV show, see if you can tell which Trigger you are seeing—do you see four white stockings, or only one?

11 FAMOUS HORSE STORIES

Some of these stories are about real horses. Some of these stories are about fictional horses. These horses were't actually real… but they can feel real to the people who love their stories. All of the stories can teach you about horses, English, people … and even yourself.

Books

Many (although not all) famous horse stories were written for children or teenagers. However, that does not mean that they have simple vocabulary or grammar! If you try one of these books in English and it seems too hard, try reading it first in your own language. Then try again in English. Every story recommended here is one I have personally read and that I recommend. Even if the language is a little hard, because it is a great story, it can be motivating to read.

- *Misty of Chincoteague* (Marguerite Henry)
- *Justin Morgan Had a Horse* (Marguerite Henry)
- *King of the Wind* (Marguerite Henry)
- *Black Beauty* (Anna Sewell) Written for adults. Told from the horse's point of view!
- *National Velvet* (Enid Bagnold) Written for adults.
- *Seabiscuit* (Lauren Hillenbrand). Written for adults. An easier book about the same horse, written for children, is called *Come On, Seabiscuit!* (Ralph Moody).

Horse series

These books all feature the same characters in each book, and are written in the same style. That means they get easier as you read more of them.

- **The Black Stallion** (Walter Farley). This is the name of the first book, but there are 24 books in this series! The same author wrote a second series about the *Island Stallion*. It's also good, but I think the Black Stallion books are better. You will learn a lot about the world of horse racing with this series.
- The **Jill** books (Ruby Ferguson). This is an older series, from the 1950s, and one of the best-loved horse series ever. The books (about a girl, her horses, and the riding club she belongs to) were so popular that you can often find used books in libraries or for sale online. They can also be

bought as ebooks and paperbacks here: https://shop.janebadgerbooks.co.uk/pages/ruby-ferguson.

- **The Saddle Club** (Bonnie Bryant). An American series about teens and their horses. There are over 100! So if you like these, you can read for a long time. The first one in the series is called *Horse Crazy*.
- The **Jinny** books (Patricia Leach). Set in Scotland. There are 12 books in this series. The first one is called *For the Love of a Horse*, and tells how the girl Jinny finds and tames a wild Arab horse.

Movies

It's no surprise that many of the famous or popular movies about horses began as books. In fact, many of the books in this section have been made into movies, including:

- *National Velvet*: The movie made from this classic book was filmed in 1944 and starred a young Elizabeth Taylor as a rider who believed her horse could win the Grand National, a famous horserace. It's considered a very well-made movie. There is a sequel, called *International Velvet*, that did not begin as a book, that was made in 1978.
- *Misty* (1961), the movie made from the book Misty of Chincoteague. A look at one special

pony from a group of wild horses who live on an island on the east coast of the US.

- *Black Beauty*: There have been at least 8 movies made from this story, as well as two TV series. The movie that most closely follows the book was made in 1994.
- *The Black Stallion* (1970) and *The Black Stallion Returns* (1983) are two movies made from this popular series.

Here are some more famous horse movies you might enjoy. If the language is hard, it's okay to turn on subtitles in your native language or in English.

- *Phar Lap* (1983), the true story of an amazing racehorse from Australia.
- *The Silver Brumby* (1993), which describes the wild horses of Australia.
- *Spirit: Stallion of the Cimarron* (2002). An animated film that tells the adventures of Spirit, a wild horse in the American west. Spirit's voice is done by Matt Damon.
- *Seabiscuit* (2003), the true story of a remarkable racehorse.
- *Hidalgo* (2004), about a cowboy who takes his horse to race in Saudi Arabia.
- *Secretariat* (2010), another true story of a famous racehorse. But if you like one, you will probably like them all!

There are also two TV series you might enjoy:

- *The Saddle Club* (1990s), based on the American books but made in Australia with Australian actors. You can find full episodes on YouTube. There were three seasons of 26 episodes each. They're easy to understand, too.
- *Heartland*, about a "horse whisperer," a Canadian girl who can communicate easily with horses. There are 17 seasons so far, with the most recent one released in 2024. In fact, *Heartland* is the longest-running one-hour TV drama in Canadian history! You will learn a lot about taking care of horses from this series.

∿

I hope you enjoyed learning more about horses!

www.ingramcontent.com/pod-product-compliance
Lightning Source LLC
Chambersburg PA
CBHW021225020426
42331CB00003B/471